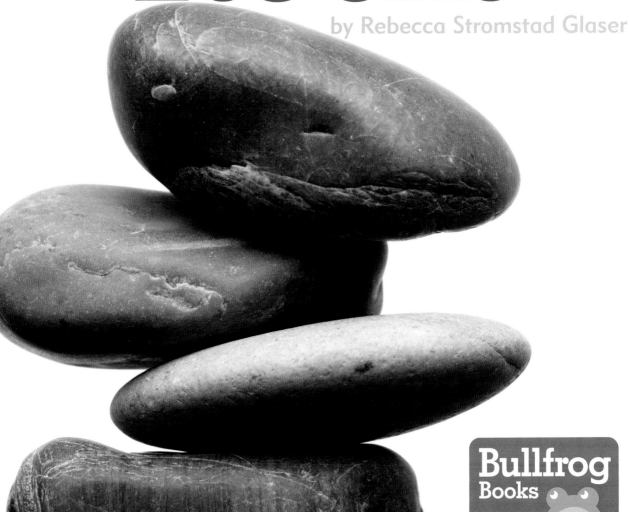

Nature Walk

# Rocks

by Rebecca Stromstad Glaser

**Bullfrog Books**

# Ideas for Parents and Teachers

Bullfrog Books let children practice nonfiction reading at the earliest reading levels. Repetition, familiar words, and photo labels support early readers.

### Before Reading

- Discuss the cover photo. What does it tell them?

- Look at the picture glossary together. Read and discuss the words.

### Read the Book

- "Walk" through the book and look at the photos. Let the child ask questions. Point out the photo labels.

- Read the book to the child, or have him or her read independently.

### After Reading

- Prompt the child to think more. Ask: What kind of rocks have you seen? Would you like to collect rocks?

Bullfrog Books are published by Jump!
5357 Penn Avenue South
Minneapolis, MN 55419
www.jumplibrary.com

Library of Congress Cataloging-in-Publication Data
Glaser, Rebecca Stromstad.
Rocks / by Rebecca Stromstad Glaser.
p. cm. — (Bullfrog books: nature walk)
Summary: "Describing different types of rocks, this photo-illustrated nature walk guide shows very young readers how to identify common rocks. Includes photo glossary"—Provided by publisher.
Includes bibliographical references and index.
ISBN 978-1-62031-028-1 (hardcover : alk. paper)
Rocks—Juvenile literature.  I. Title.
QK432.2.G53 2013
552—dc23

2012009108

Series Designer: Ellen Huber
Book Designer: Heather Dreisbach
Photo Researcher: Heather Dreisbach

Photo Credits
Dreamstime, 1, 3b, 4, 5, 6, 10-11, 14–15, 20tl, 20b, 21, 23ml, 23tl; Getty Images, cover; Science Photo Library, 16; Shutterstock, 3t, 7, 8, 9, 10, 12–13, 14, 17, 18-19, 19, 20tr, 23bl, 23tr, 23mr, 23br, 24

Printed in the United States of America at Corporate Graphics in North Mankato, Minnesota.
7-2012 / 1123
10 9 8 7 6 5 4 3 2 1

# Table of Contents

# Looking for Rocks

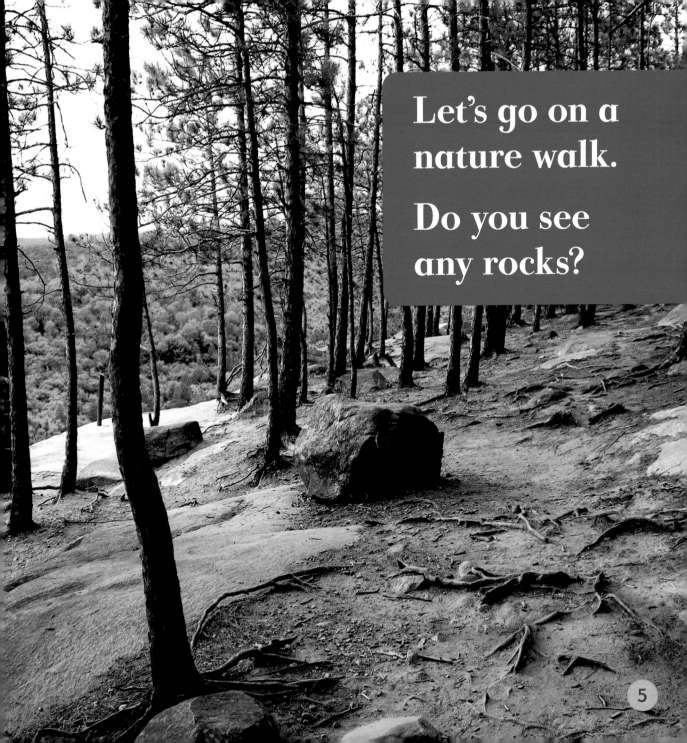

Let's go on a
nature walk.

Do you see
any rocks?

Look along a river.
Water wears
away the rocks.
River rocks
are smooth
and round.

**Look in a field.**

# A boulder is rounded. It is big.

Look for a fossil.

It is very old.

It is an imprint
of a plant or
animal.

fossil

# What is this rock?

It is petrified wood.

It is old.

The wood changed into stone.

Look for flint.

It can spark to start a fire.

**Look for a geode.**

geode

16

crystals

It is round and hollow.
Crystals are inside.

Look for granite.

It is bumpy.

It has three or
more colors.

The grains
are minerals.

# What rocks have you seen?

# Rocks and Fossils

**ammonite**
A spiral shell fossil from an ancient sea animal that was like a squid.

**sandstone**
A kind of rock made up of tiny grains of quartz and other rocks.

# Picture Glossary

**flint**
A hard rock that sparks when it is hit with steel.

**granite**
A hard rock made of the minerals feldspar, quartz, and mica.

**fossil**
A plant or animal from millions of years ago, preserved as rock.

**mineral**
A substance found in nature; minerals make up rocks.

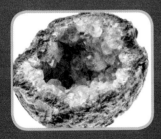

**geode**
A round rock lined with crystals inside.

**petrified wood**
Dead wood that has turned into stone because chemicals have seeped into its cells.

# Index

# To Learn More

Learning more is as easy as 1, 2, 3.

1) Go to www.factsurfer.com

2) Enter "rocks" into the search box.

3) Click the "Surf" button to see a list of websites.

With factsurfer.com, finding more information is just a click away.